THE Quilted
PORTRAIT BOOK

Teri Henderson Tope

The American Quilter's Society or AQS is dedicated to quilting excellence. AQS promotes the triumphs of today's quilter, while remaining dedicated to the quilting tradition. AQS believes in the promotion of this art and craft through AQS Publishing and AQS QuiltWeek®.

Director of Publications: Kimberly Holland Tetrev
Assistant Editor: Adriana Fitch
Project Editor: Sarah Bozone
Copy Editor: Caitlin Tetrev
Graphic Design: Lynda Smith
Cover Design: Michael Buckingham
Photography: Charles R. Lynch

Additional copies of this book may be ordered from the American Quilter's Society, PO Box 3290, Paducah, KY 42002-3290, or online at www.ShopAQS.com.

Text and designs © 2015 Teri Henderson Tope
Artwork © 2015 American Quilter's Society

Library of Congress Cataloging-in-Publication Data

Tope, Teri Henderson, author.
  The quilted portrait book / by Teri Henderson Tope.
    pages cm
  ISBN 978-1-60460-212-8
  1. Machine quilting. 2. Portraits on quilts. I. Title.
  TT835.T659 2015
  746.46--dc23
                            2015029866

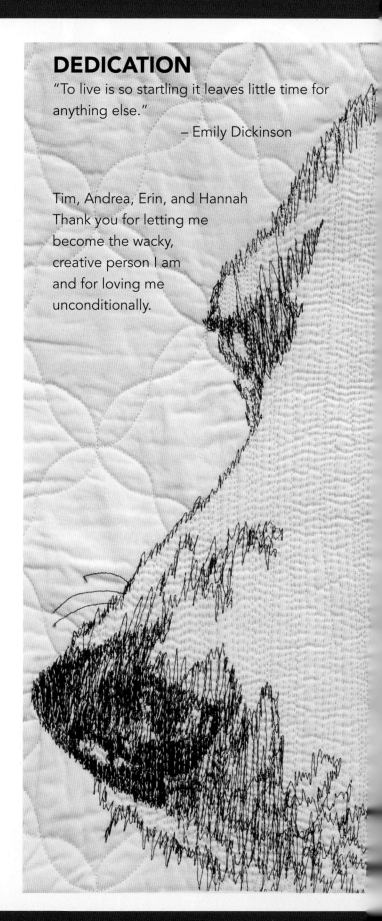

DEDICATION

"To live is so startling it leaves little time for anything else."

— Emily Dickinson

Tim, Andrea, Erin, and Hannah
Thank you for letting me
become the wacky,
creative person I am
and for loving me
unconditionally.

TABLE OF CONTENTS

INTRODUCTION

I have a box in my sewing studio. In that box are the treasures I have collected over the years. It contains photos, quilt pictures torn from magazines, a birthday card or two, and even a scrap of wrapping paper. It contains images that speak to me—inspiration I held on to for a rainy day.

One rainy day I pulled out that box. As I shuffled through old photos and scribbled drawings, I came upon a photo of my three daughters. The photo was taken when the youngest was only three, she is now 17. These three beautiful, smiling, happy faces are my muses.

I believe we all have that special image, caught on film, as if by magic. It is the one special photo that pulls at your heart. I wanted to recreate my version of that image and capture that fleeting moment in time. On my home sewing machine, with reinforced fabric, black thread, and an embroidery hoop (to keep the images flat), I began stitching the pre-drawn images. I chose to create these images in black and white to enhance the shadow/contours of the portraits. Slowly, the features appeared. More thread was stitched and before I knew it I could recognize my girls. I was planning my next portrait before I finished the first.

I've been asked why I choose black and white for this technique. Why not add color? I want to create a unique look and, quite frankly, something a little different. I also love seeing the image emerge, quick and easy, by just adding more thread and creating contour with shadows. It is addicting.

This book will guide you step by step through my process. Soon you will create your own stylized version of a thread portrait.

> Note – Please read all instructional information before starting. There are tips and explanations of the how and the why to successfully create a quilted portrait using my technique.

SUPPLIES

Fabric

- 1 yd. light-colored, tightly woven cotton fabric
- 1 yd. white fusible cloth backing (such as Sew Lazy Face It: Soft, Lightweight Fusible Interfacing by Lazy Girl Designs™ or Pellon® SF101 Shape-Flex® interfacing)
- Fabric for backing, borders, piping, and binding
- Wool batting

Thread

- 1 cone black thread (such as Superior® So Fine!) with at least two pre-wound bobbins
- Thread for machine quilting completed project can also use black cone thread

Machine Foot

- Free-motion or hopping foot
- Walking foot

General Supplies

- 10" wooden embroidery hoop or 7" spring tension embroidery hoop
- 16½" square ruler
- Blue water-soluble fabric pen
- Extra sewing machine needles (such as Microtex Sharp 80/12 from Schmetz Needles®)
- Iron and Ironing board

- Bath towel
- Light box
- Piping Hot Binding with Groovin' Piping Trimming Tool by Susan K. Cleveland
- Rotary cutter and cutting mat
- Seam ripper
- Scissors
- Sewing machine with feed dogs that can be dropped
- Quilter's pins
- T-Pins

Optional
- Cone holder for thread
- Thread Portrait Kit

■ The Photo

Choose a photo that is well lit. This technique enhances the shadows of the photo. Too many shadows will create a very dark portrait. This will work, if a very dark portrait is what you are going for. A photo that is too bright may leave no shadows and create a flat looking portrait. Images must be in focus. Blurry or even slightly blurry images do not enlarge well and you will find it difficult to trace on the light box.

If the photo is taken in color, no worries, it can be manipulated in your photo software to gray scale or black and white. Import the photo into a design program, such as Adobe® InDesign® or the program that you use for your digital camera.

Then switch the image from color to gray scale or black and white. Does it still have the same impact? I once had a student choose a beautiful blue clematis flower for her project. When the image was changed to black and white it simply did not have the same impact as the color version. This is why I choose faces/portraits for this technique, as they tend to convert beautifully without losing impact. I can add amazing contrast just with black thread.

Many photo programs give you the ability to edit your photo. Play around with the contrast of the photo. I wish I could give you a formula on how to do this, but each photo is different. The goal is to enhance the shadows without losing the features.

You might also be able to adjust the brightness of the photo image.

I originally called this technique "Shadow Play", because the emphasis of the thread on the fabric was to enhance the shadows, not to show the exact edge of the image. The shadows are what give my portraits the contour needed to make them appear more dimensional. The stitching of the black thread, either thinner and looser or tighter and closer, create the visual imagery of the line. This is an artistic reproduction of the photo, not an exact copy.

Once the image is adjusted, you will want to crop parts that are not necessary and enlarge the image.

I enlarge the image to make it easier to stitch the detail. Smaller images have less detail and fewer shaded areas. They also require fine line detail and can be a bit more challenging. My favorite/average portrait size is about 14" to 18" on the longest side. My design program will adjust the remaining side to the appropriate measurement. Eighteen inches (18") is also an easy size to stitch using your home sewing machine, without much twisting and turning of the fabric.

To print your pattern, you can send it via email to a professional/quick printer. They can print it on one sheet. Ask for a lightweight paper. It will be easier to see through, on the light box, in the next step. Call the printer ahead of time to check their computer image requirements. You can also print the pattern on your home computer printer and tape the pages together to create the finished pattern. I usually send mine to a printer, because the patterns tend to use a large amount of toner/ink. This way I do not have to worry about the taped edges.

■ The Fabric

Fabric for the quilted portrait should be of a light color. You will be spending much of your time stitching thread onto your portrait. Dark or patterned fabrics take away from the stitched line. Lighter solid fabric will let all your hard work shine.

Fabric should be of high thread count and tightly woven. Muslin or lightweight fabrics are not suitable. We will be stitching a great deal of thread onto this fabric. Thin fabrics could develop holes and uneven tension creating more wrinkles or puckers in the finished portrait. Fabrics, such as decorator fabrics, are too heavy to see through. This makes the transfer of the image more difficult.

I suggest you use Northcott's Colorworks line. I have seen students create beautiful quilts using light colors, such as soft peach and soft yellow.

Borders – This is where you can have a little fun, if you wish. The borders of the quilted portrait are sewn in a quilt-as-you-go technique. I tend to use solid black fabric for my borders, but my students have done some beautiful, colorful border treatments.

Piping – Piping is also added to my portraits. I love how it looks like extra matting, like around a framed picture. I use Susan Cleveland's Groovin' Piping Trimming Tool to add that little bit of style to my portraits.

■ The Stabilizer

There are many stabilizers on the market that would work with this technique. I choose Sew Lazy Face-It: Soft. It is a soft, fusible, lightweight cotton backing that gives nearly invisible support to the quilter's cotton used for the quilted portrait. It adds great stabilization to the fabric, helping to keep better tension during stitching and therefore less wrinkles. You also need to add this stabilizer to the fabric for extra support when stitching. Quilters cotton fabric is just too to thin for the amount of thread needed to create the portraits. Face It Soft is pliable and therefore easier to hoop during portrait stitching.

■ The Thread

The thread you use in your quilted portrait is as important as the fabric you choose for this project. I suggest Superior Threads King Tut Quilting Thread in Black. King Tut is an extremely low-lint #40/3 extra-long staple Egyptian-grown cotton thread. Extremely low lint means you'll spend more time quilting and less time cleaning out your machine. It's a thick thread that can easily be seen as you stitch and it creates great solid black coverage when needed. Purchase it on a cone, you will thank me. . . we are going to use a lot of thread!

I choose to use black thread, as it enables me to create the light, medium, and dark coverage need to create dimension in the portraits. I have tried brown or sepia colored thread and just did not get the desired result.

Bobbins – Before you get started you are also going to wind a few bobbins. Fill the with the same or lighter weight thread to be used in your quilted portrait. Or purchase prewound bobbins. They hold a lot more thread and are easy peasy to just grab and install.

> *Tip – Keep that little sewing machine brush handy. Clean out the bobbin area after every bobbin change. Your sewing machine will thank you*

Cone holder – If you choose to use a cone of thread you will want to check your sewing machine to make sure you have the capabilities to use one. If not, I suggest you use a cone holder that is specially designed to hold a cone of thread. My students have struggled with

uneven tension by using makeshift items to hold their cone of fabric. This is just a suggestion, but I want you to have a good experience while stitching your portrait.

■ The Sewing Machine Needle

The needle I choose is a Microtex Sharp 80/12. It is perfect for the King Tut thread. It is a very thin, acute point creates beautiful topstitching and perfectly straight stitches for thread work when precision is paramount.

> *Tip – Change the needle on your sewing machine every couple of hours. During the free-motion stitching process needle will become dull or possibly bent.*

Changing the needle will keep your machine running smoothly and your stitches even.

■ The Hoop

In order to stitch our quilted portraits, we will need a hoop to stabilize the fabric. I use a 7" spring tension hoop or a 10" wooden hoop (see picture) The hoop needs to be able to fit under your hopping or free motion foot. I prefer the 10" German made hardwood hoop. I was told by a very talented friend to cover the inner ring with ½" twill tape, which I glued the loose end down with a tiny bit of hot glue. This gives me just enough grip to keep my fabric in place.

I also love the added couple of inches of stitching area it gives me. Thanks Beth Schilling.

■ The Light Box

You will need a light box to trace the pattern onto your prepared fabric. Students have tried to trace on a window or by constructing a makeshift light box from a lamp/light and plexiglass/box. We will be tracing through the paper pattern, stabilizer, and fabric. Truthfully, you will need a light box to be able to see properly and get good results. I realize this is a big expense, but the makeshift light boxes will not get the job done and it will end in frustration.

■ Marking The Fabric

Water-soluble marking pen – I use a Clover® Blue Water-Soluble, medium-marking pen to trace the pattern onto the prepared fabric. A fine line marker is often hard to see and sometimes fades. As you will see in the stitching process, I also use the pen to color in areas in need of a little more thread.

> *Tip – Purchase a new pen at the start of your project. Through experience I have had the pen dry up or run out of color halfway through the transfer process (usually at an inopportune time, in the middle of the night, when a trip to the local quilt shop is out of the question).*

■ Blocking The Fabric

T-pins – We will be using t-pins to block our project when stitching is complete. This is after we rinse all the blue water-soluble markings from the fabric. The smooth T-bar shaped head and sharp pointed tip will easily penetrate the blocking surface without bending.

■ The Batting

Wool batting is the great equalizer for this project. During the stitching process there will be some areas that do not contain any thread. Upon completion these areas tend to contain a bit of fullness. Wool batting, along with the quilting, eases this fullness. You will also have fewer wrinkles or puckers in the completed project. We will be adding quite a bit of thread coverage so the wool batting is a dream to quilt through. This will create less stress on you and your machine.

■ Painter's Tape

Painter's tape adheres to fabric without leaving a residue. This makes it perfect for attaching the paper pattern to our prepared fabric. It comes in handy when hanging your paper pattern for easy viewing during the stitching process.

■ Iron & Ironing Surface

What quilting studio is complete without a good iron and ironing surface? We will be using the iron to press all creases from the fabric before getting ready to begin the portrait. This will be the only time you press during the stitching process, so you will want to start with your fabric as flat as possible. Ironing will also come into play when we prepare the finished portrait for quilting the addition of the borders.

■ The Sewing Machine

The sewing machine stitch is the most important key to the successful completion of a quilted portrait. The quilted portrait requires a sewing machine that has free motion capabilities, a free motion foot, hopping foot or darning foot, and the ability to drop the feed dogs. Portraits are sewn using reinforced fabric in a hoop. I stitch on a BERNINA 750 QE with a knee lift. The knee lift allows me to pivot slightly without taking my hands off the hoop during the stitching process. Please check or sample stitch on your machine to determine stitching capabilities before starting your quilted portrait. All tension issues should be resolved and sample stitched using the prepared fabric placed in the hoop. Working out these issues before getting started will create a tension free work zone. You will

CREATING THE QUILTED PORTRAIT

also need a walking foot to quilt the portrait. This will create even channel quilting to help ease any extra fullness created in the stitching process.

Prepare your photo for portrait and print it out.

Cut a piece of fabric about 8" bigger than your printed pattern. This allows for 4" on each side. The extra fabric is needed to properly hoop the portrait during the stitching proces.

Next, cut a piece of Face-It: Soft the same size or slightly smaller than your portrait pattern fabric. Follow the manufacturer's directions to fuse the stabilizer to the back of your portrait fabric. Make sure you press it well and have good adhesion. The project will not be pressed again until we are finished with the stitching process. We will be tracing the image on the fabric with the blue marking pen and will not want to heat set the markings.

■ Sample Practice Block

Use the sample block to test the fabric, sewing machine tension, and to practice before beginning your portrait.

Using the scraps of the remaining fabric and stabilizer, cut a block approximately 8½" x 11" from both pieces and fuse per manufacturer's directions. I have supplied a couple of easy images for you to trace onto this prepared block for practice.

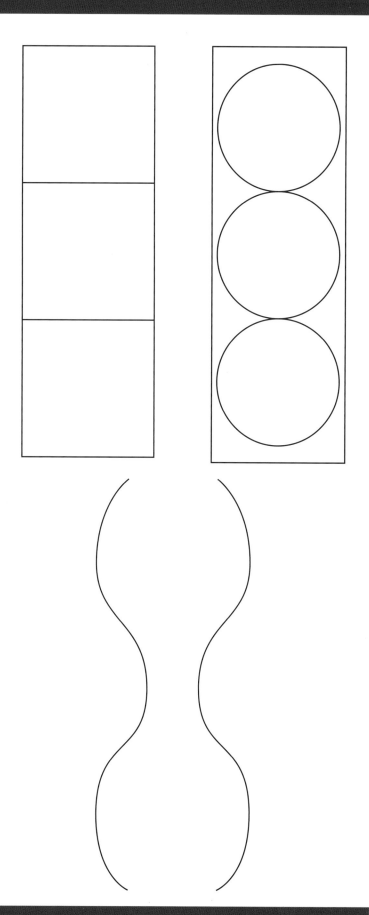

▪ Preparing the Fabric

Center the right side of the printed paper pattern against the wrong side of the prepared stabilized fabric. This will result in the right side of the pattern facing the stablizer.

Take the painter's tape and tape the edges of the pattern to the wrong side of the prepared block. I do not pin the pattern to the fabric. Pins tend to wiggle around and get caught on hands and elbows during the tracing process.

▪ Tracing the Image

Plug in and turn on the light box.

Place the prepared pattern/fabric piece over the light box with the taped paper pattern side against the light box.

On the right side of the fabric, trace the edges of all shapes you see with the blue pen. Mark every shadow, light and dark. The result will look like a crazy cartoonist, paint by number drawing. Do not be afraid. This is what the portrait is suppose to look like.

If you are having problems seeing through the prepared fabric and pattern, try turning off the ambient lighting around the room. This tends to help me see more detail. Trace as much detail as possible. These lines will be our registration lines and will be washed out upon completion of our portrait. The more registration lines the better.

Trace the sample block patterns onto the prepared 8½"x 11" block.

When you have completed the tracing, carefully remove the paper pattern and fold the tape over the edge of the pattern. Do not try to remove the tape from the pattern, as it will tear. Reserve this pattern. We will refer to it during the stitching progress. Look closely at your traced fabric. With a marking pen, adjust or add any lines or shapes you may not have been able to see through the pattern while on the light box. Place the pattern within easy viewing of your sewing area, so you can refer to it as you stitch.

▪ Stitching the Practice Block

Thread the sewing machine, attach a free motion or hopping foot, and drop the feed dogs. You do not have to set a stitch length, as we are going to free motion stitch. Thread the machine with black thread.

Hoop fabric – I always start with my practice block. To properly hoop your fabric, place the outer hoop rim on a flat surface. Place fabric right side up over the outer hoop. Next, put the inner hoop over the fabric and gently push it into the inside the outer hoop. Fabric should be taut, with no wrinkles, and it should be laid against the flat surface with hoop facing you.

You should not have to pull to adjust the fabric. If you pull to adjust the fabric, you might pull too much and create uneven tension, creating wrinkles when your portrait is unhooped.

The Stitching – Start stitching at the center edge of the practice rectangle.

Pull bobbin thread to the top of the fabric. Pulling bobbin thread to the front keeps knots and tangles from forming on the back of your project. It makes it easier to clip off threads as you go.

Fill in the first square by stitching from the center edge to the top and back down to the bottom as if you are using an Etch-a-sketch®.

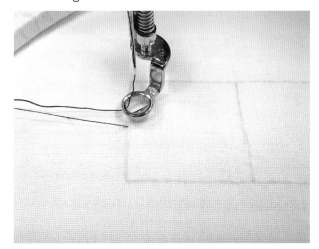

Clip off threads as you go to keep your sewing surface free of tangles. I try to start in the center of a line, stitch out to the point, then back to the starting point, to prevent having a thread dangling from the start of a line or shape. When the needle touches the bottom edge, immediately stitch back leaving a small point as you go.

Continue stitching from the top to the bottom of the block filling it in. The lines of stitching should be about ⅛" apart, but remember this is just practice, so no worries if they are closer or farther apart. Try to create small, even stitches. Notice how well the stitched line shows up on the fabric, creating a dark line. Large stitches will raise when uphooped. You do not have as much control on larger stitches. Find your perfect speed to create controlled stitches. Start slow. Students have expressed their desire to rush due to the sheer volume of thread that has to be stitched to complete the portraits. Stitches that

are too small will create a nest of fabric on the front and back of your fabric.

We start in the center so that we do not have to tie off or backstitch the thread. You could start your thread by taking a few micro-stitches. After you stitch the first block, do not remove your thread, but continue stitching into the second square. Try to make these stitching lines closer together, so that it looks darker than the first square. On the last square, stitch to achieve a full thread coverage. You may want to go over it and stitch to get the desired result. A gradation of color should appear.

Sewing Stitch Fingerprint – I believe, after having taught this technique many times, that each sewist has their own style of free motion stitching. Some will be feathery light and others will be very heavy handed when stitching their unique portrait. Both will be successful, if they are consistent in their stitching. This is a uniquely personal sketching-with-thread technique. It is you and the machine creating the line, shape, and shading into a work of art.

Stitching negative spaces (rectangle with circles) – The next practice image will help you learn to fill with curved lines.

Reposition the fabric in the hoop to center the rectangle with the circles.

Drop the needle in center of the outer edge and stitch to fill in around the circles, stopping at edge of rectangle. This is a lesson in backtracking over previously stitched areas. The goal is to not see the crossover stitching.

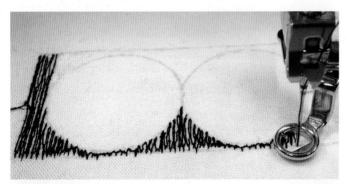

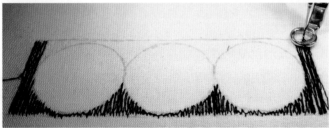

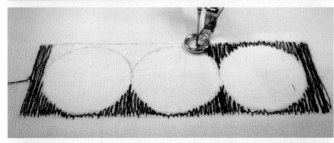

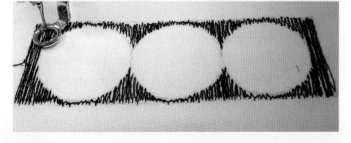

Stitching Straight Lines – Straight lines take a bit of practice. Straight lines, outlines, and small creases all require just a little bit of stitching, a light touch. I have found that stitching a wiggly line that I refer to, as a bad EKG, tends to give the portrait the hand sketched look I desire. I feel a perfectly straight line looks out of place or draws your eye to it. This makes other areas look messy or not well stitched.

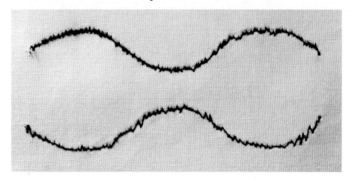

■ Stitching on the Quilted Portrait

After successfully stitching the practice block, it is time to hoop and begin your quilted portrait.

The biggest question is always, where to start. In this technique there is no hierarchy of order. This means it is not necessary to start from the center and work outward. If you make sure the prepared fabric is hooped properly you will have no worries.

> *Tip – Make sure the stabilizer is facing the wrong side of the prepared fabric. The color of the fabric and the color of the stabilizer are often very close to the same shade and easy to mix up.*

Stitch the darker areas. Load the traced, prepared fabric into the hoop. I get the best results by stitching the darker areas first. After creating dozens of these amazing portraits, I still tend to be a bit nervous starting out. I always begin in a less conspicuous place, such as hair or clothing, to get my balance and courage.

Top to Bottom Motion – Even stitching is the key to this project. You do not have to stitch quickly. These works of art take a little time and a great deal of thread. Slow and steady wins this race. Relax and get into a rhythm. I tend to lose tack of time at this point. Stitches that are sewn top to bottom in a somewhat straight line create a uniform look throughout the portrait upon completion.

If you are having problems reading the traced pattern, use the blue pen to fill in darker areas. We will be rinsing these marks out completely. I tend to do this when stitching the eyes, ears, mouth, and nose and to create definition in curls or highlights in the hair.

FEATURES

Each portrait is unique. Remember this is an artistic interpretation of the original image. This is not an exact duplication. The audience, viewing your portrait, will not be seeing the original image. There is room for artistic license.

■ Eyes

Look at your pattern closely. Notice dark, medium, and light areas. Forget the standard visual image of an eye.

Look at what you have drawn. It may not look anything like an eye, as an image all by itself, but when the portrait is finished the eyes became true.

Start out with a light coverage of thread. It is easier to add more thread as you go, constantly editing your thread coverage. I often go back to a particular feature a couple of times, as the portrait emerges.

■ Nose

My experience stitching with noses is LESS IS MORE.

Stitch nostrils very lightly, constantly editing as you go.

Stitch the bare minimum of the nose. Revisit the nose as you progress, comparing it with thread coverage on the remaining portrait. You can always go back and add more detail.

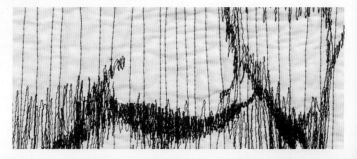

■ Mouth and Teeth

Again, LESS IS MORE. Try not to outline every tooth or you will get a "Howdy Doody" looking smile. The hint of an outline of a tooth goes a long way.

Use a light or medium thread coverage for the lips. They should have a "shine" or light area.

Be sure to leave the light area, because it will give the lips contour and make them less flat.

■ Ears and Face Outline

In the quilted portrait, the ears and edges of cheeks, neck, and face are often hidden or blended with the background. The light catches the edge with just a hint of shadow. This is where you might want to grab that blue pen and do a little creative drawing. Refer to your paper pattern for guidance or, if needed, your original photo.

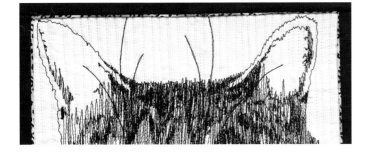

Using the bad EKG type line, stitch a subtle edge, leaving spaces in the line (not a continuous line). Again, use a very light touch. You can always add a bit more shadow.

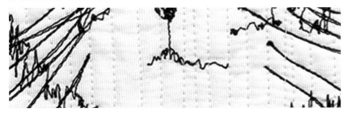

■ Glasses, Jewelry, and Other Additions

With a very light touch, stitch dark areas or shadows of the images only.

Leave light areas alone. Do not outline completely.

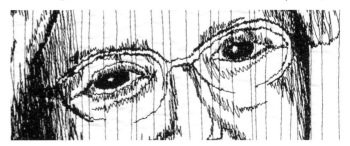

Look at the pattern. Notice the shadows and the highlights. You will get a more interesting visual image if you stitch with a light touch. Your eye will automatically complete the line.

BACKGROUND

Adding Background – I have included in this book several portraits with and without backgrounds. The key to a successful background is semi-straight stitching. Do this part of the quilt last. During the stitching process you will need to move the hoop around, stitching in an uneven pattern, so you don't leave a hard line across the background.

> *Tip – Occasionally as you add stitching to your portrait, you may find that your fabric will pop out of the hoop. This is caused by the coverage of the thread on the fabric. If you cannot keep the fabric in the hoop, and it keeps popping out, release the tension of the hoop by turning the small screw. If you are using a spring tension hoop, after hooping the portrait, gently fold the edges of the fabric over the top edge of the hoop to ease the threadwork into the hoops groove.*

Portrait edges, at this point, will be very uneven and you may have a puffy spot or two in unstitched areas. We can address these in the blocking and quilting stage.

When is the portrait finished? I often have a hard time stopping when stitching a portrait. I have found that if I walk away from it for a few hours, then revisit it, I can look at it with a fresh eye. An added line here, a bit more shading there, and eventually the portrait will tell you that it is done.

FINISHING

You will want to do this next step in one session. So allow an hour or two to rinse and block the quilt.

■ Rinse

Upon completion of all the threadwork, it is time to remove all the blue markings from the portrait.

Fill a clean sink with warm water.

Loosely roll the quilt and gently place in the water. Press down on the quilt to completely saturate it with water. Turn the quilt over in the water.

Press repeatedly to move the water through the quilt. Do not wring water from the quilt.

Lay a clean bath towel on a flat surface. Unroll the quilt on the towel and flatten it. It will be very lumpy and puffy. We will easily deal with this during the blocking stage. Our goal is to remove as much of the water, as possible.

Roll the flattened quilt in the towel from the top of the quilt to the bottom. Press down on the towel to dry the block.

Unroll and then re-roll the quilt from side to side. Press down on the towel when rolled. You may need to use a second towel.

When the quilt is damp dry, it is time to block it. This will remove the lumpy and puffy areas and will straighten areas that have constricted during the rinsing process.

■ Block

To properly block the quilt you will need T-pins and a surface they will easily pierce, so the quilt remains stable. I use a very dense piece of foam core (two boards glued together) to block my quilts.

Place the quilt on the surface and run a line of pins across the top of the block.

Grasp the bottom of the quilt and gently pull down, stretching the quilt while placing a row of T-pins across the bottom. We will be constantly moving these pins so do not worry if the project is not flat on pinning.

Next place a row of pins down one side. Gently tug the quilt and place pins on the opposite side.

Now that the sides are roughly pinned, we can start working on the problem areas. Take your time during this process.

Gently stretch the quilt top to the bottom and side-to-side removing and replacing pins as you go. Lumpy and puffy areas should slowly ease out. The quilt should become semi-flat. Remember we will also be quilting our project. The quilting will help remove fullness from unstitched areas on the quilt.

When you have stretched and tugged to get a semi-flat piece, the next step is to let it dry completely, at least 24 hrs.

■ Quilt

I use a quilt-as-you-go technique to quilt my portraits. This step should be done in one sitting. You do not want to unpin your blocked quilt until you are ready to quilt. My Ohio summers are hot and humid. If I unblock my portraits without quilting them, they revert back to a lumpy, puffy mess.

Un-pin the blocked portrait. If necessary, press it with a steam iron from the back. The edges of the quilt will be ruffled in some areas. We will be cutting down the edges and hiding some of them in the seam allowances.

Place the quilt on the rotary mat. Using a square ruler and fabric marking pen (blue water-soluble or chalk) mark the outer edge of your quilt.

When the edge is marked using a ruler and a rotary cutter, trim the excess fabric ½" from this line. Leave a ½" seam allowance around edge of the portrait. Again, this edge may be a bit ruffled.

■ Borders

Decide how wide you would like the borders to be on your portrait.

Measure your portrait block and cut a piece of backing material that is 4" larger than your block and border measurements combined.

Cut a piece of wool batting the same size as your backing fabric.

Place the portrait block over the batting. Measure to center with a ruler.

Using quilters pins, pin baste portrait to the batting and backing. You do not need to go overboard with the pinning. We are going to manipulate the portrait to remove excess lumpy areas. Pin in a ½" seam allowance area and pin three (3) or four (4) areas in the middle of the quilt.

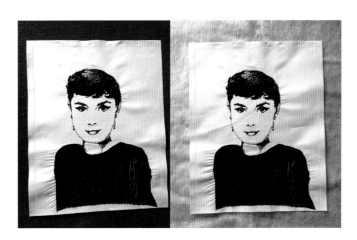

I have included examples of quilting with thread matching the background and quilting with black thread (the same thread used in the thread work). Each color usage adds a unique design element to the portrait. It is your amazing piece of art. It is your choice for the quilting. The black thread looks great on old photos and creates a sepia type finish. Matching thread to the fabric lightens up really dark portraits. I put the same thread in the bobbin that I will be using to quilt the top of the portrait.

Place walking foot on the sewing machine and set the stitch length at about 2.5. This would be a great time to engage needle down capabilities, if you have them. We will be stitching from top to bottom then bottom to top, starting and stopping, on the marked edge of the portrait. I do not draw or mark the quilting lines, but choose to free style them. I do not worry that they are not ruler straight or evenly spaced. I feel this enhances the free motion style of the threadwork used to create the portraits. As good as I think I am, if I tried to make them all exactly even and straight, there would be one that would be off and it would make me crazy.

Begin stitching one line down through the center of the portrait, starting at the top marked edge and stopping at the bottom marked edge.

Do not end the thread. Keeping the needle down, pivot the portrait.

Stitch on the marked edge to the center area left or right of the center stitched line.

Now stitch from the bottom to the top. Continue in this manner, stitching top to bottom and bottom to top, filling in channels, closer and closer together. You may want to use a stiletto to gently push or move fabric to ease bulkier areas and to prevent pleats or puckers with the quilting. You will love how the wool batt fills in the lumpy puffy areas.

Adding Piping and Borders – Piping adds a nice design element to the portrait and sometimes just the right touch of color. It looks like the matting used when framing a portrait. I use Susan Cleveland's Piping Hot piping ruler and a piping foot designed for my BERNINA when preparing piping for my portraits.

Place quilted portrait on flat surface and using a square ruler, re-mark the outer edge of the portrait, if necessary. Sometimes during the quilting process the marked edge of the portrait will become a little distorted. Be safe, re-measure and re-mark. If you are adding piping, stitch it to the portrait by placing it on the newly marked edge of the quilt.

Measure and cut the borders for the sides of the quilt and stitch.

Press the side borders. Measure and stitch the top border to the quilt and press.

Borders can be left unquilted or quilted. The suggested quilting guide ratio for wool batting is 9". Each adds another design element to the finished portrait. I have done them both ways, as seen in the examples included in this book.

Finish your quilted portrait by adding the binding and a label.

DESIGN GALLERY

This is my favorite section of any book and especially this book. I had the pleasure of guiding several groups of talented quilters through the Quilted Portrait process. Each portrait is as unique as the person creating it and each used a treasured photo. I witnessed the excitement as simple thread on fabric developed into recognizable and stunning interpretations of those favorite images. I have also included a few of my own works.

HUDSON
Made by Teri Henderson Tope
Columbus, Ohio

MY TREASURES
Made by Teri Henderson Tope
Columbus, Ohio

Earl & Ro Ro
Made by Teri Henderson Tope
Columbus, Ohio

Ray
Made by Teri Henderson Tope
Columbus, Ohio

Roxie
Made by Teri Henderson Tope
Columbus, Ohio

Andrea and Molly
Made by Teri Henderson Tope
Columbus, Ohio

JOHN, Christmas 1949
Made by Wendy Bynner
Dublin, Ohio

ANNIE
Made by Teri Henderson Tope
Columbus, Ohio

LET'S GO SAILING
Made by Faith L. Pfalz
Fort Myers, Florida

HANK
Made by Rhoda Helmuth
Plain City, Ohio

HANDI
Made by Carol Graham
Columbus, Ohio

THREAD SELFIE
Made by Teri Henderson Tope
Columbus, Ohio

COWBOY
Made by Carolyn Hageman
Port Charlotte, Florida

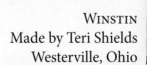

WINSTIN
Made by Teri Shields
Westerville, Ohio

MAX
Made by Alison Moffit
Dublin, Ohio

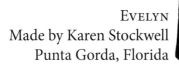

EVELYN
Made by Karen Stockwell
Punta Gorda, Florida

Some Intensions AKA Ten
Made by Teri Henderson Tope
Columbus, Ohio

MIRIAM
Made by Beth Schillig
Columbus, Ohio

AUDREY HEPBURN
Made by Teri Henderson Tope
Columbus, Ohio

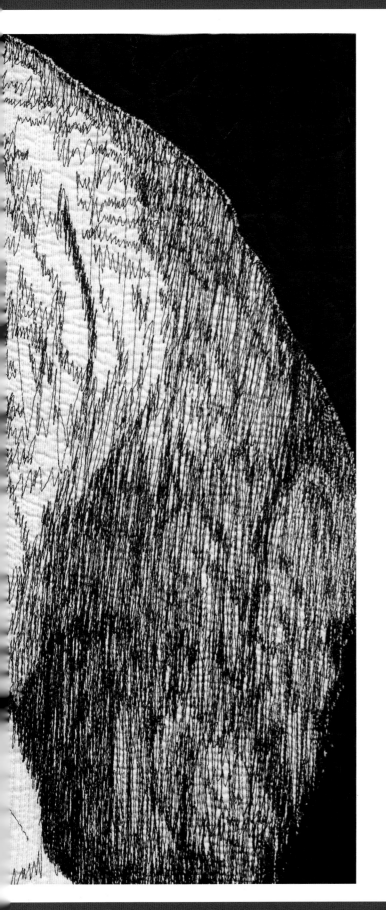

ABOUT THE AUTHOR
Teri Henderson Tope

As I write this, I realize, that in my short life, I have accomplished a great many things. A portion of that has to do with this book and my career as a professional quilter. I have made a great many quilts that had the honor of hanging in national and international  quilt venues. I have even won a ribbon or two. I have written and produced a line of patterns through my company MaTERIal Girl Designs, taught and lectured across the United States and even ventured over seas. I have authored three books with The American Quilter's Society: *Appliqué in Reverse, Home Sewn Celebrations*, and the *Bag It* book. I have filmed for Quilting Arts TV and can be found on The American Quilter's Society's iQuilt Network. I have even judged a few quilt shows. What I wish really wish for you to know is my love for my family and my love for simply stitching beautiful creative things. My family is the foundation that lets me do all the things that I do. I am not truly happy unless I have a needle in hand. My mind never stops. On occasion when I have trouble sleeping, my go to visualization is to put a quilt block together. Quilting is as much a part of me as my skin and bones. My wish for the reader of this book is that, for some small speck of time, they enter my creative, crazy world. Life is too short so go be creative!

#7262

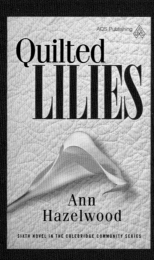

#1697

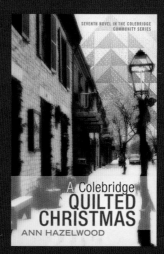

#7274

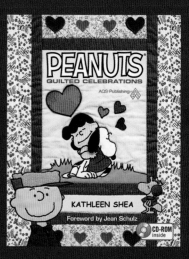

#1696

More AQS Books

This is only a small selection of the books available from the American Quilter's Society. AQS books are known worldwide for timely topics, clear writing, beautiful color photos, and accurate illustrations and patterns. The following books are available from your local bookseller, quilt shop, or public library.

#1698

#7265

#5730

#1692

Look for these books nationally. **Call** or **visit** our website at

www.americanquilter.com

1-800-626-5420